Artbook

OrangeBooks Publication

1st Floor, Rajhans Arcade, Mall Road, Kohka, Bhilai, Chhattisgarh - 490020

Website:**www.orangebooks.in**

First Edition, 2024

ARTBOOK

Rhea Gupta

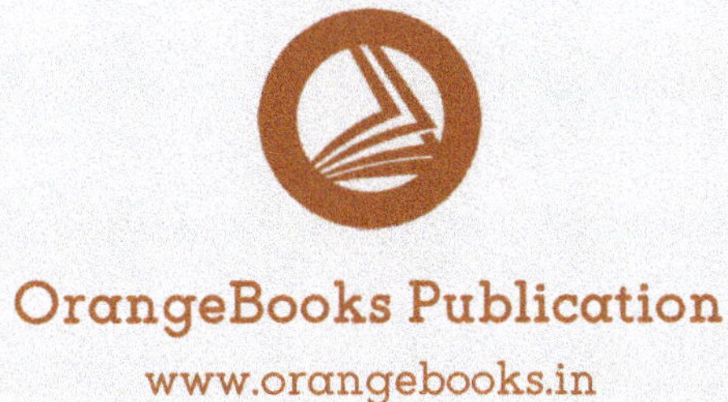

OrangeBooks Publication

www.orangebooks.in

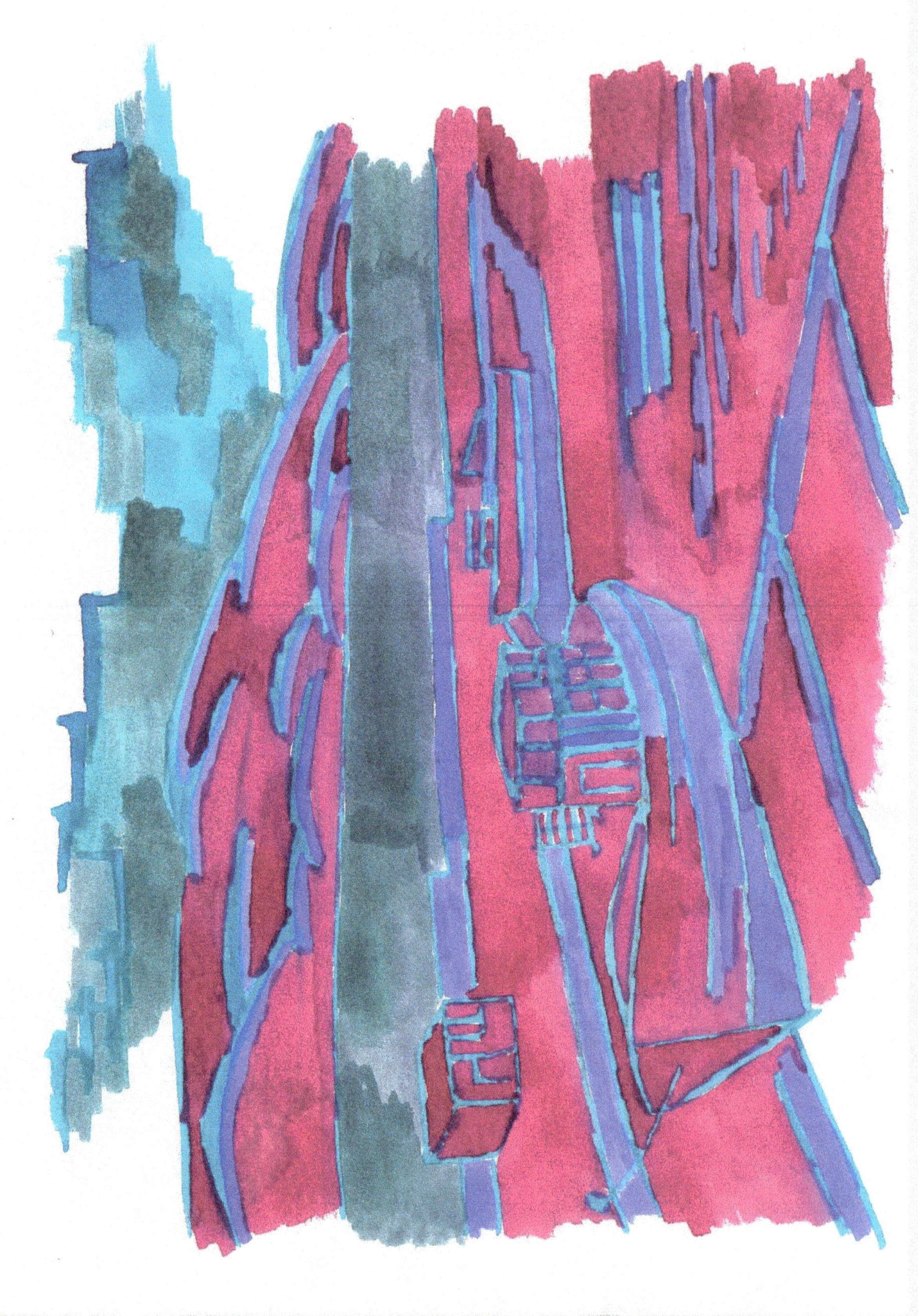

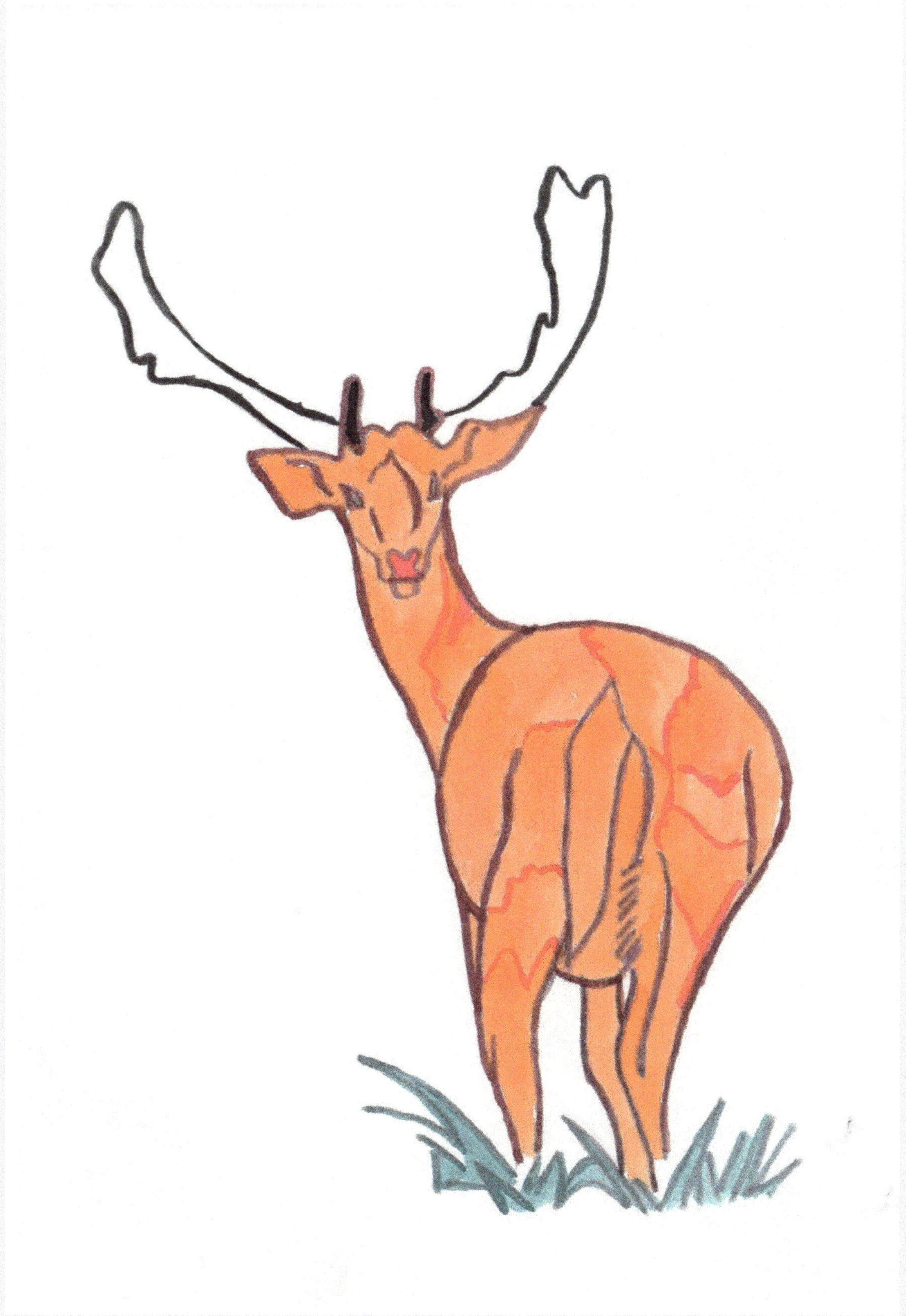

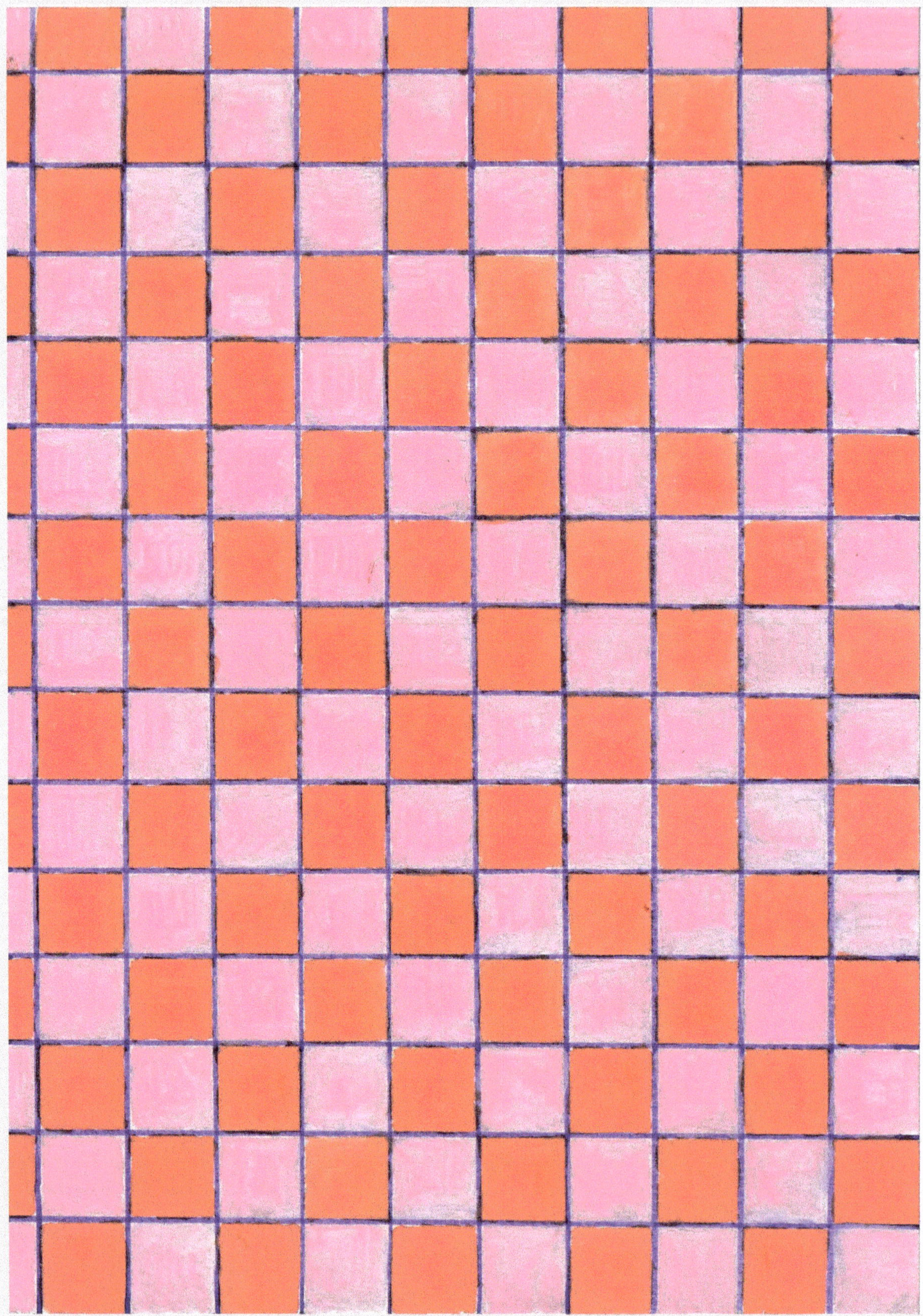

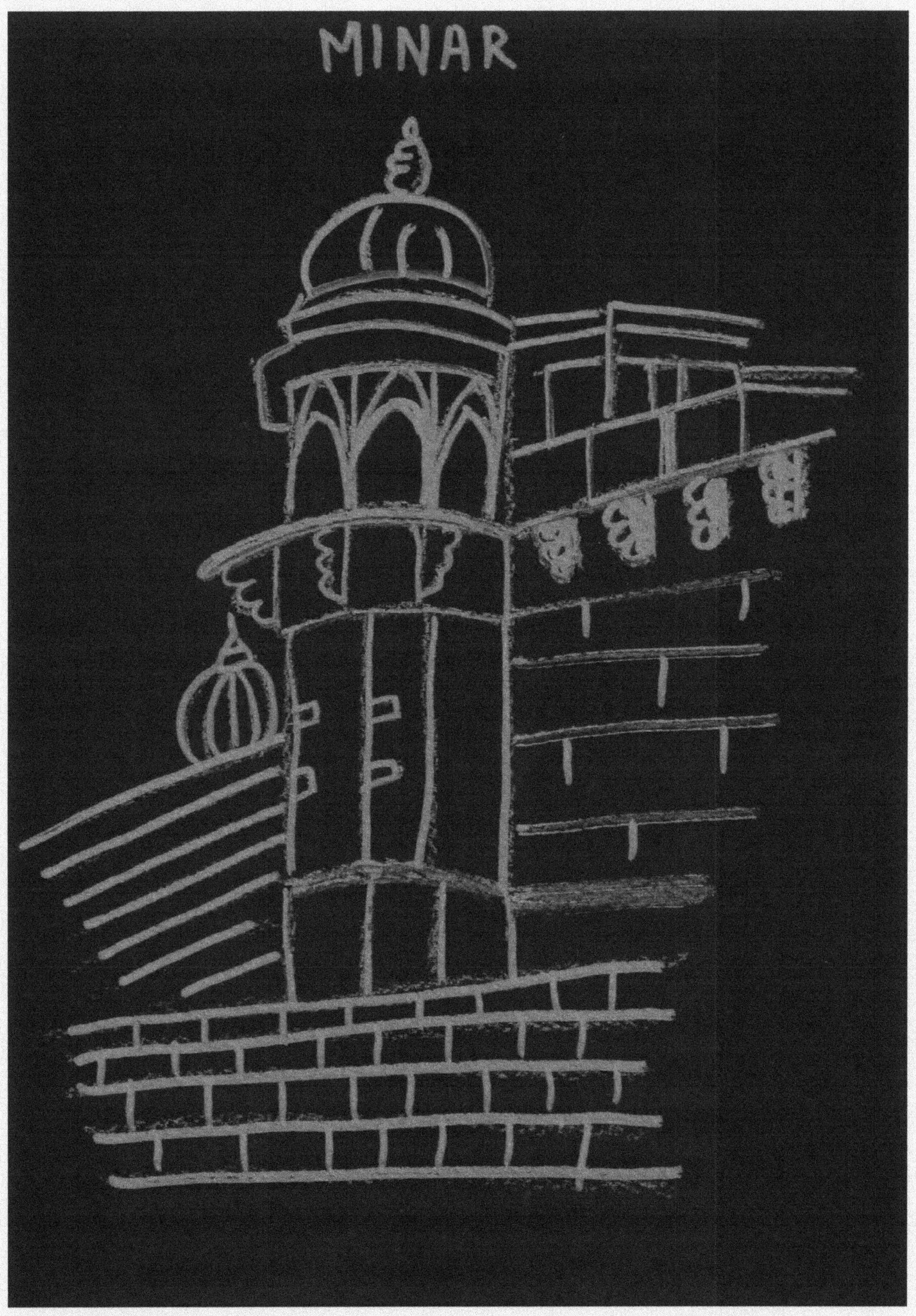
MINAR

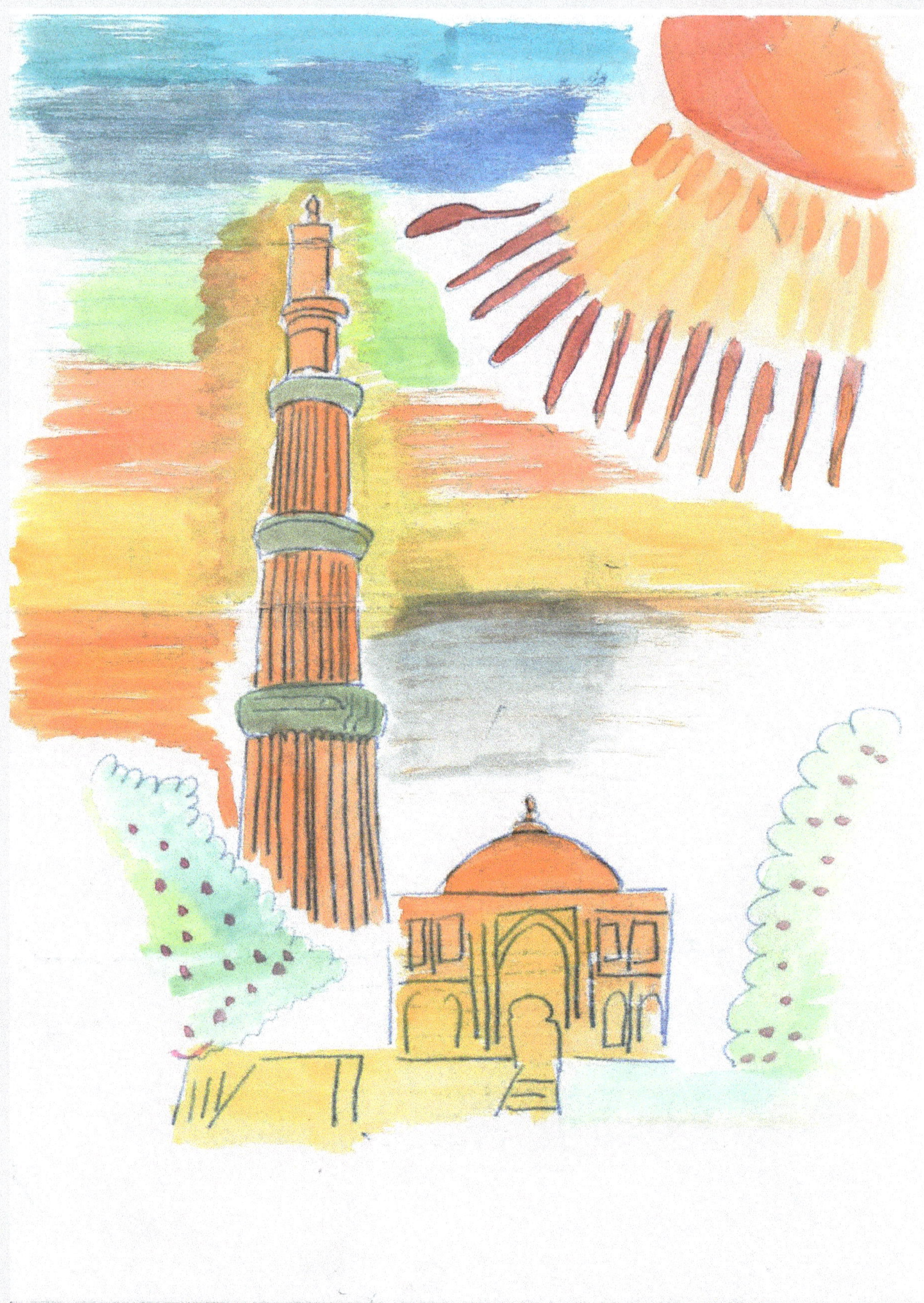

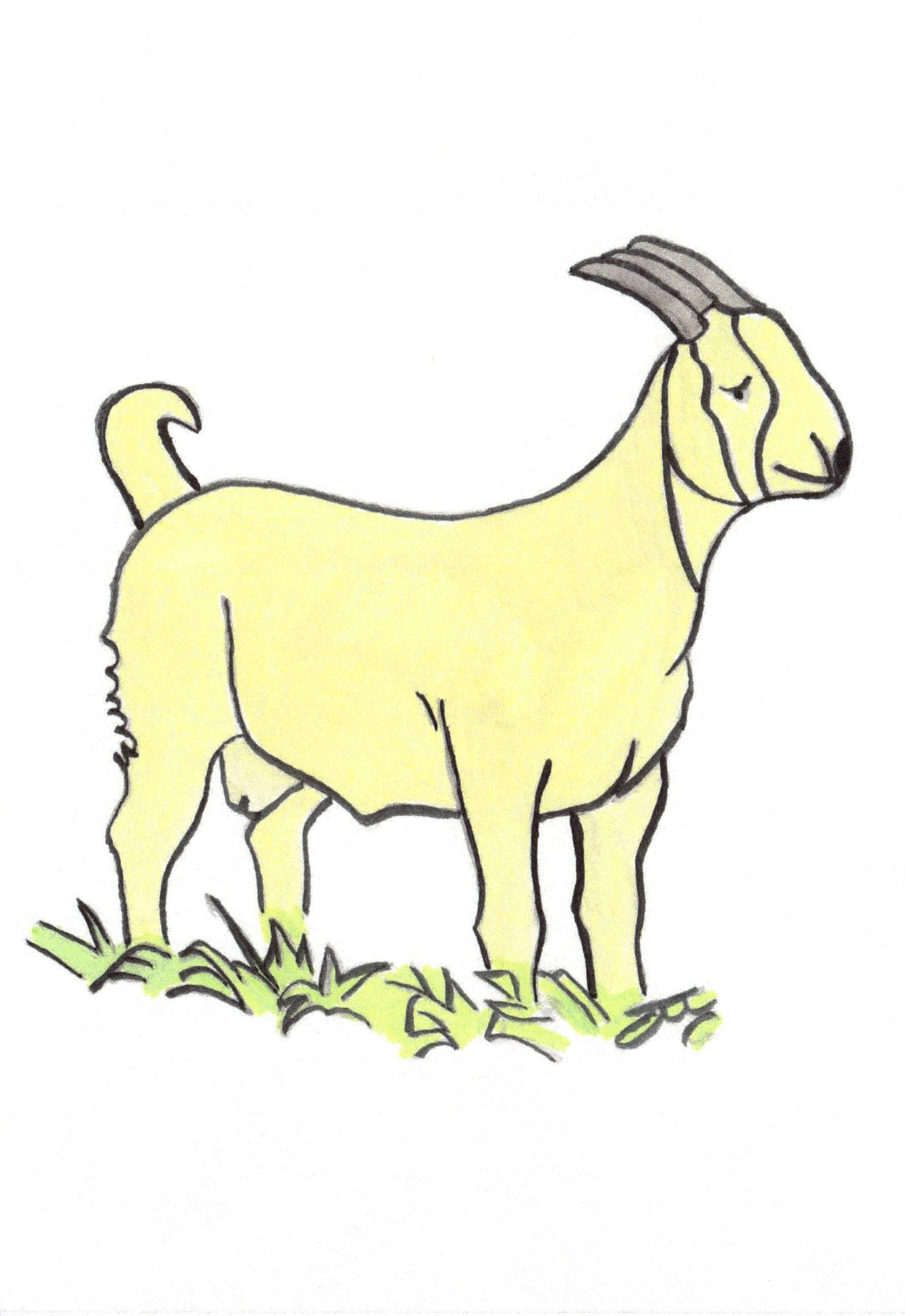

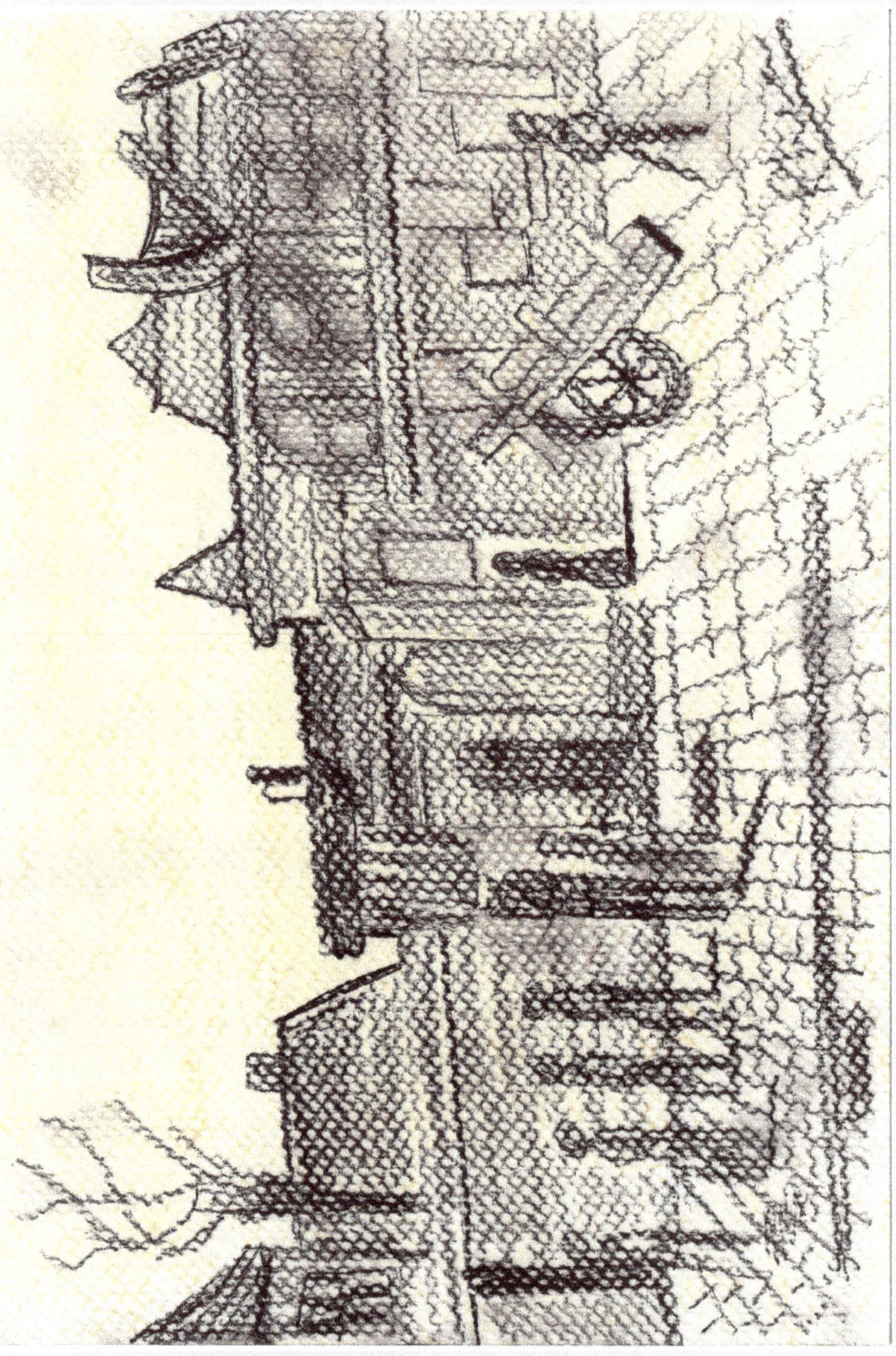

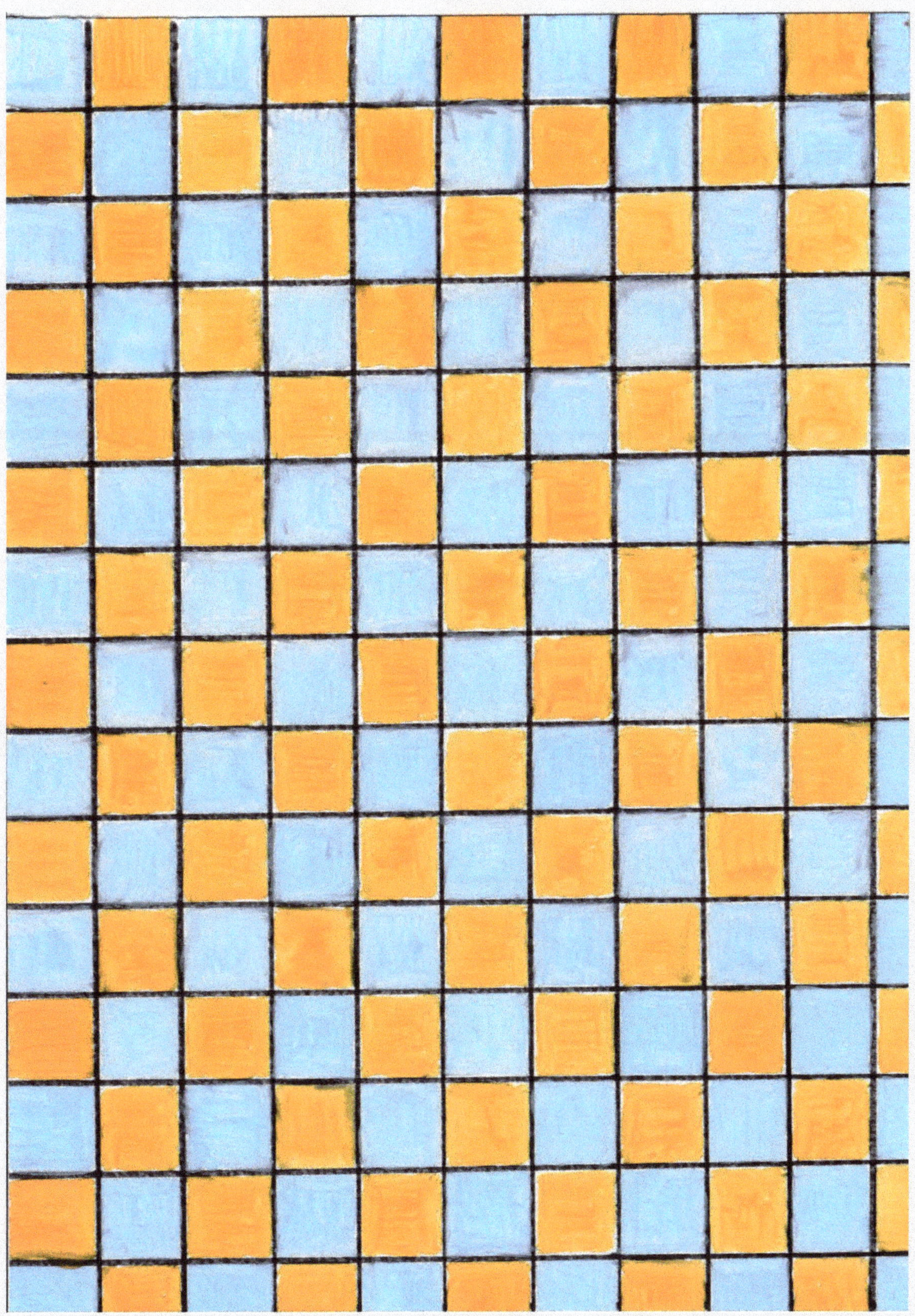

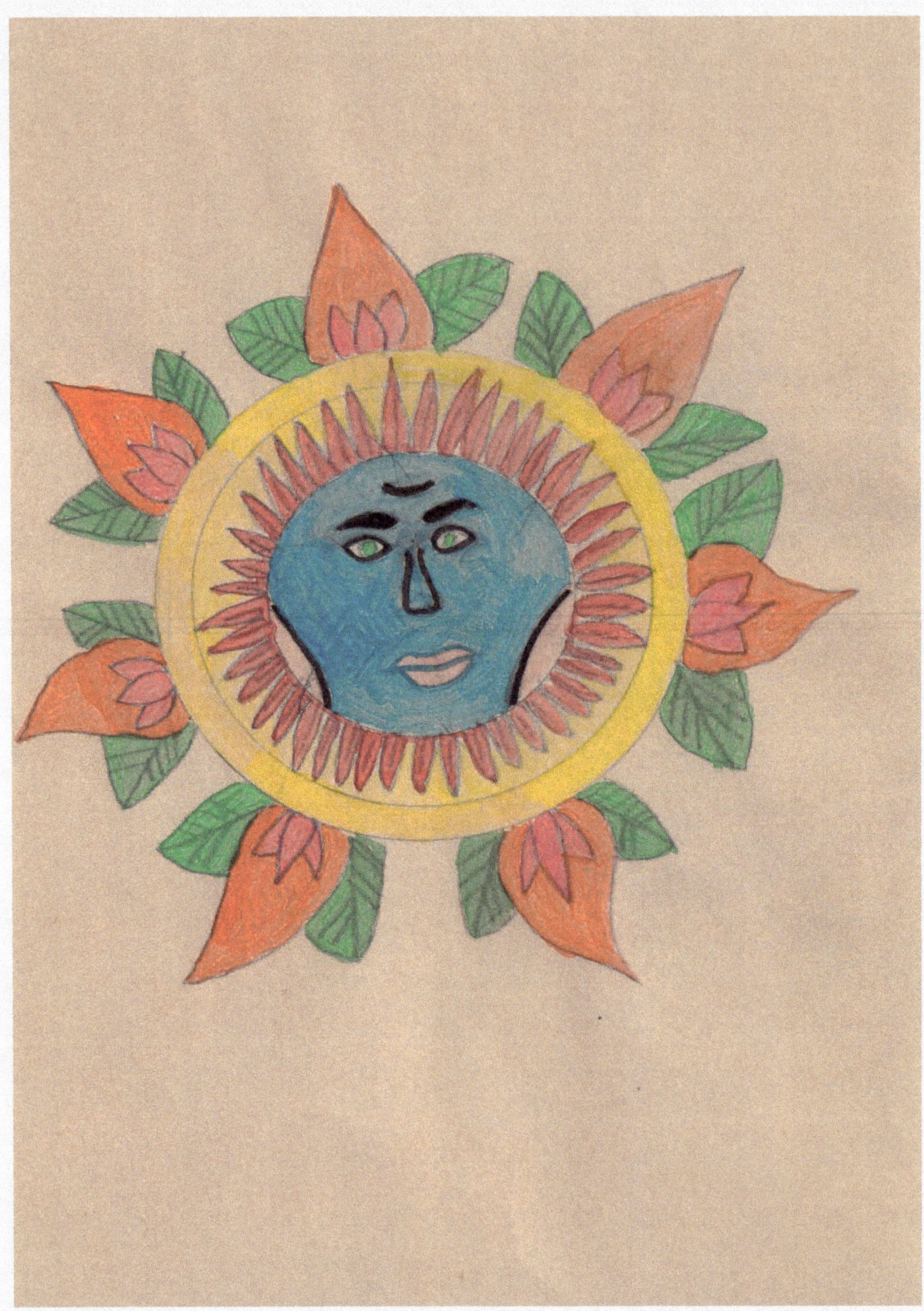

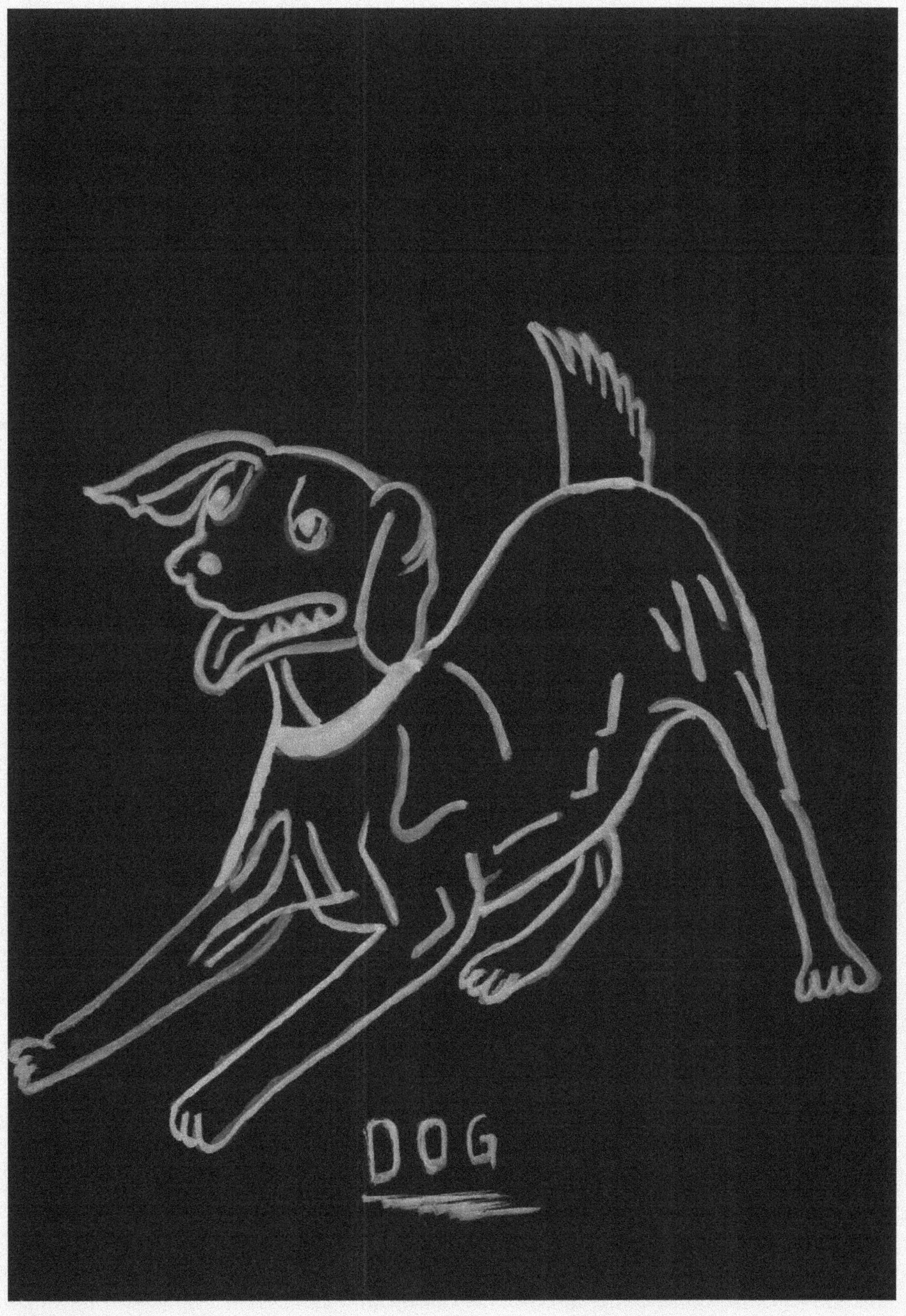
DOG

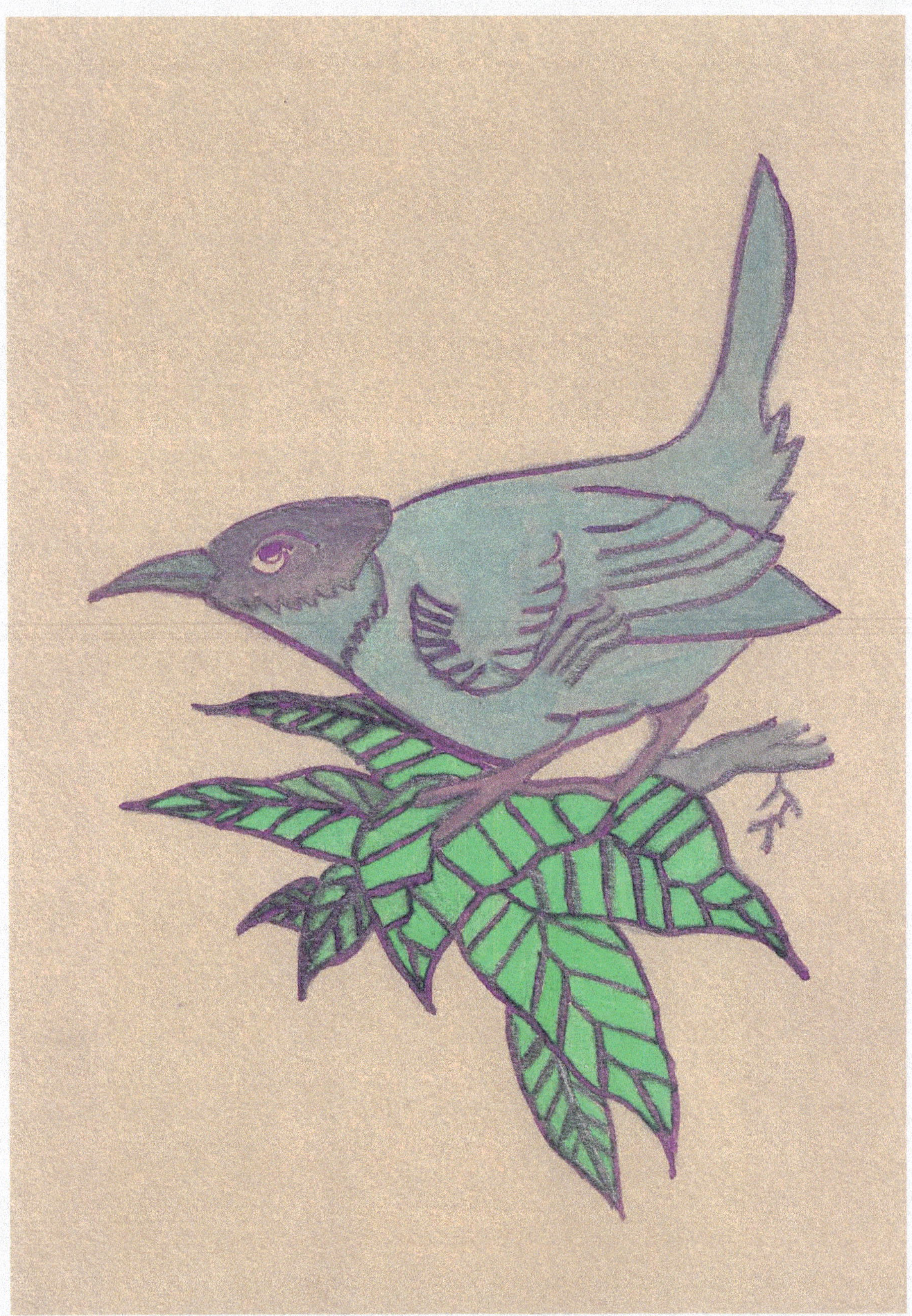

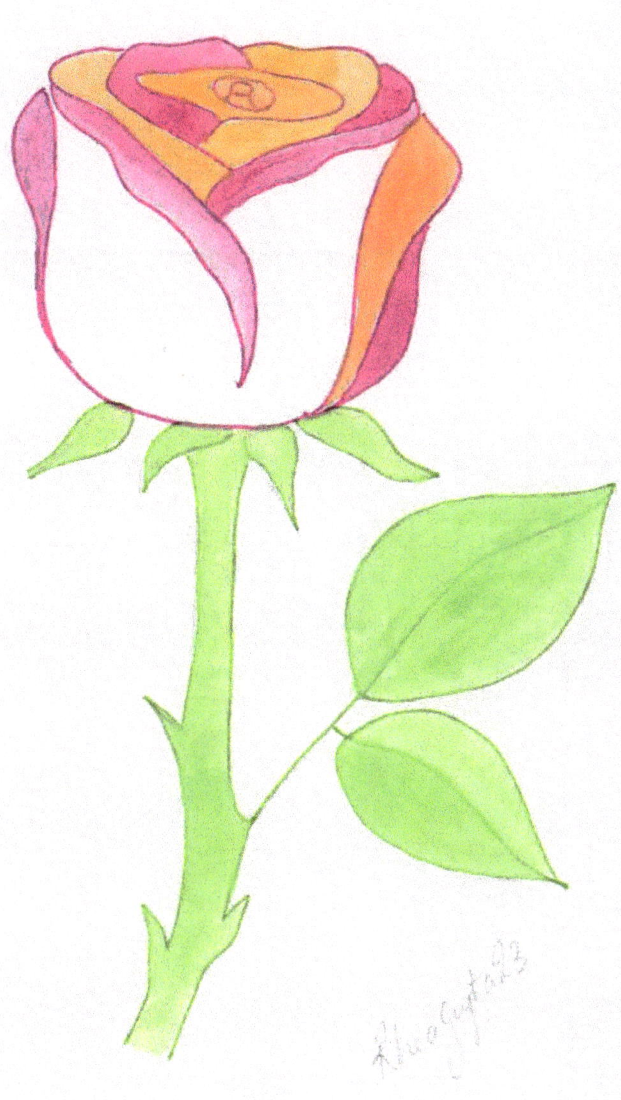

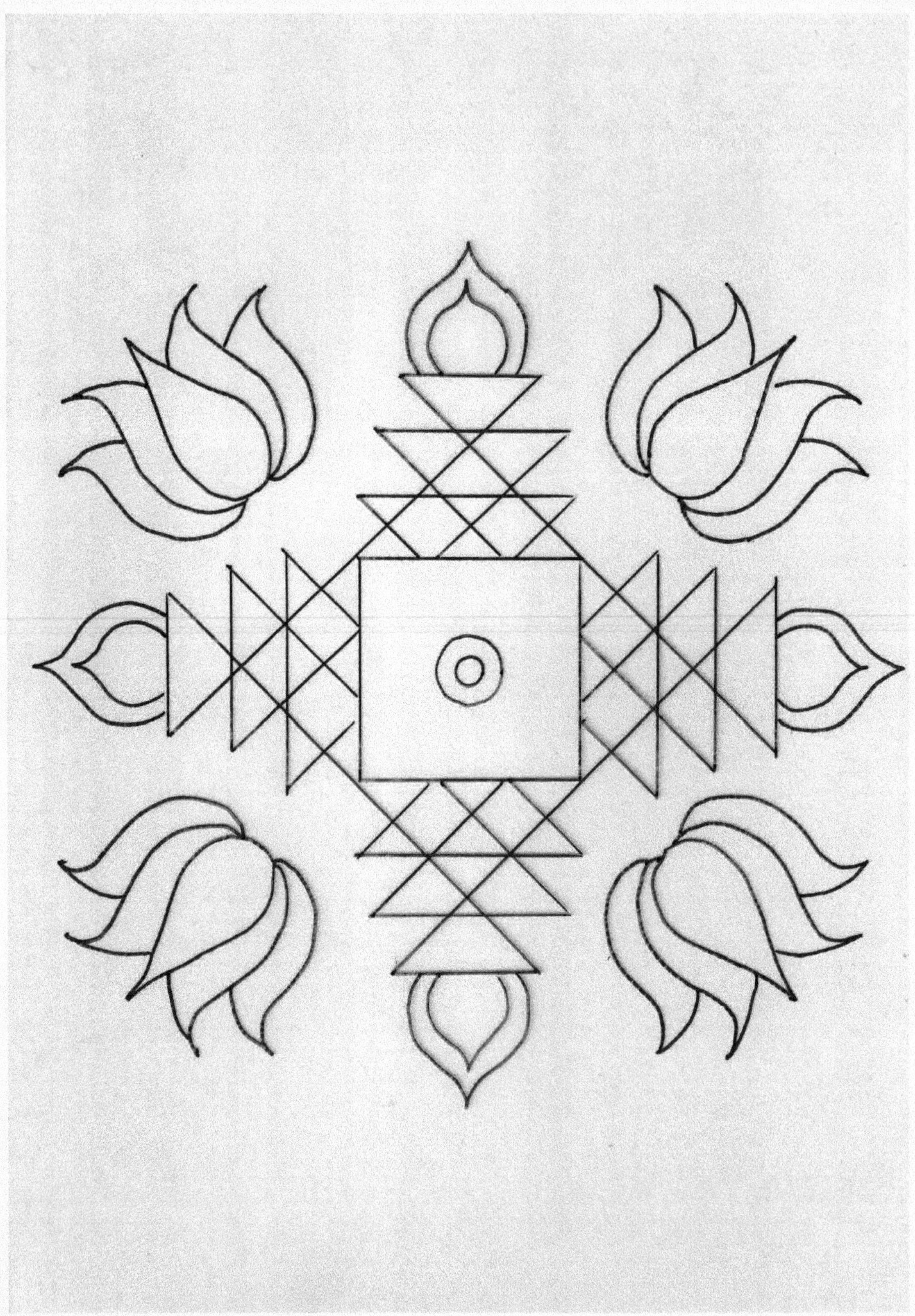

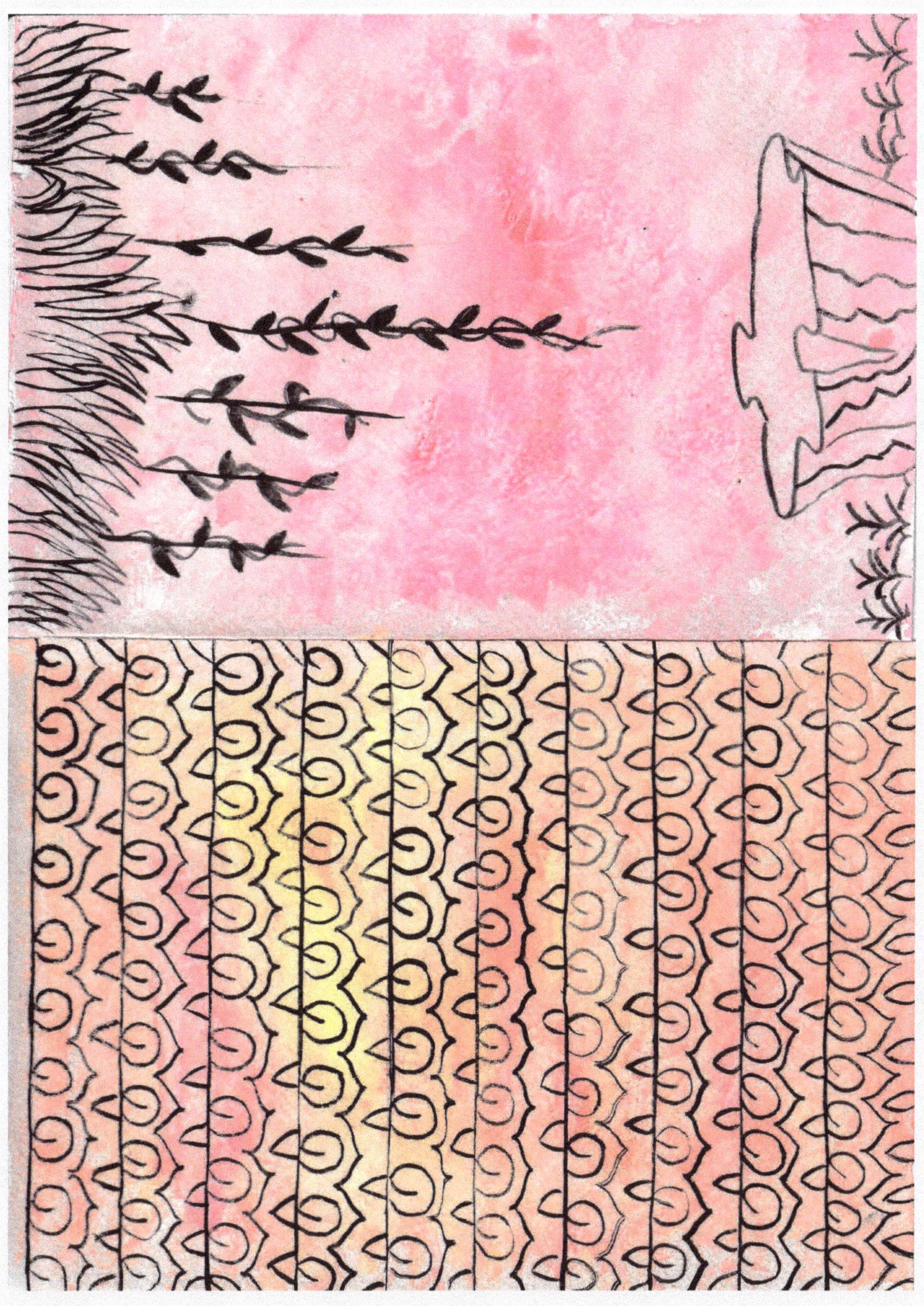

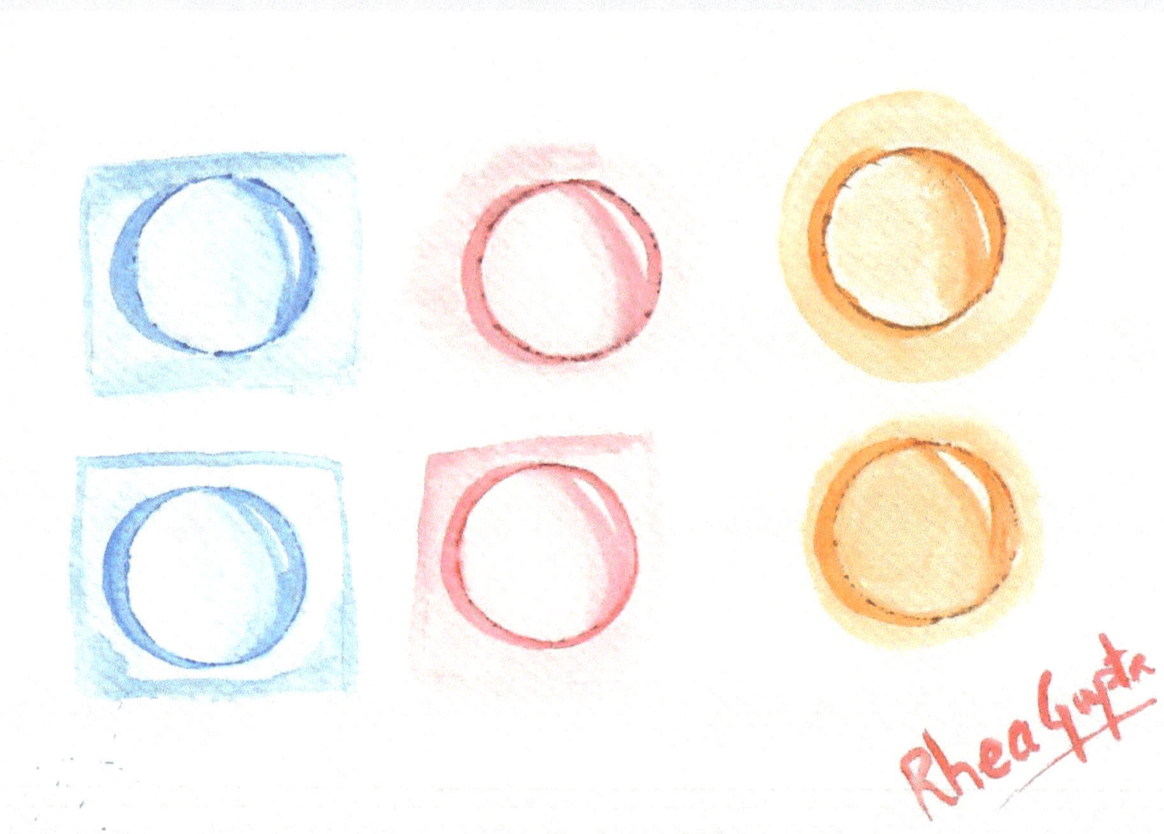

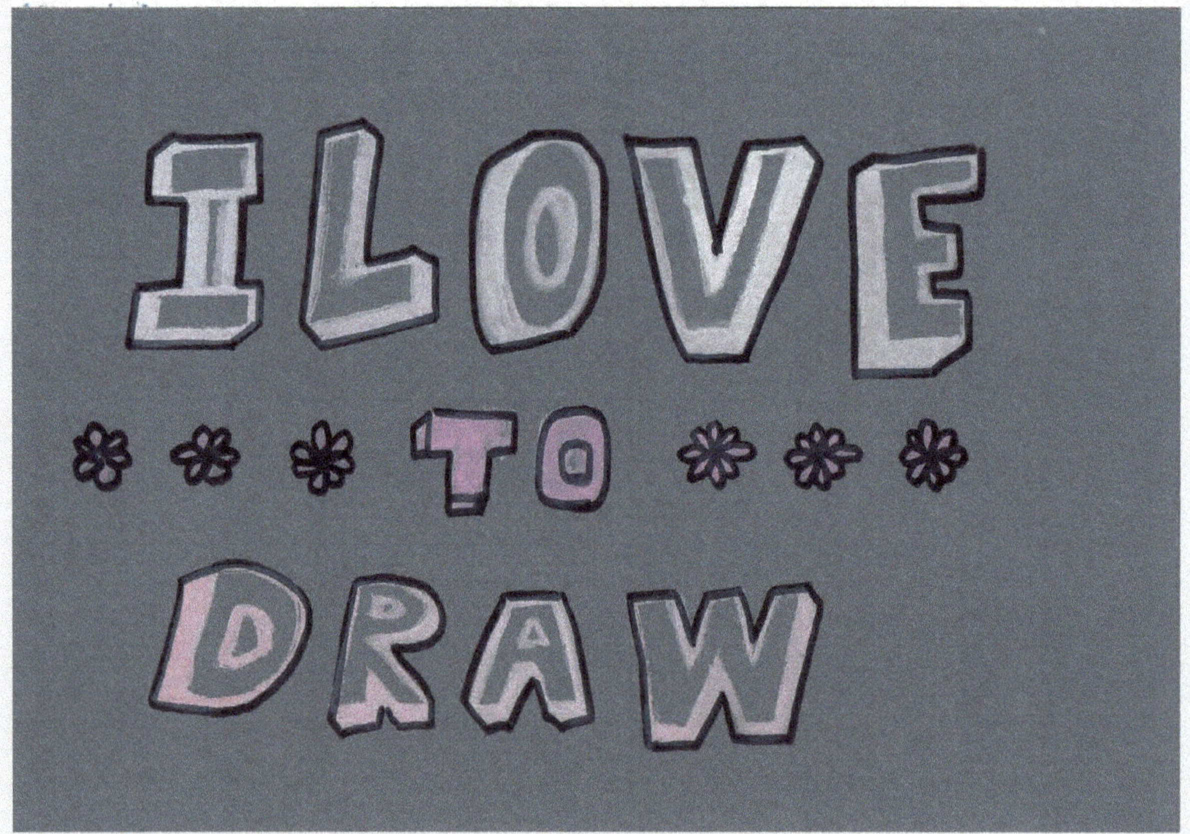

I LOVE
TO
DRAW

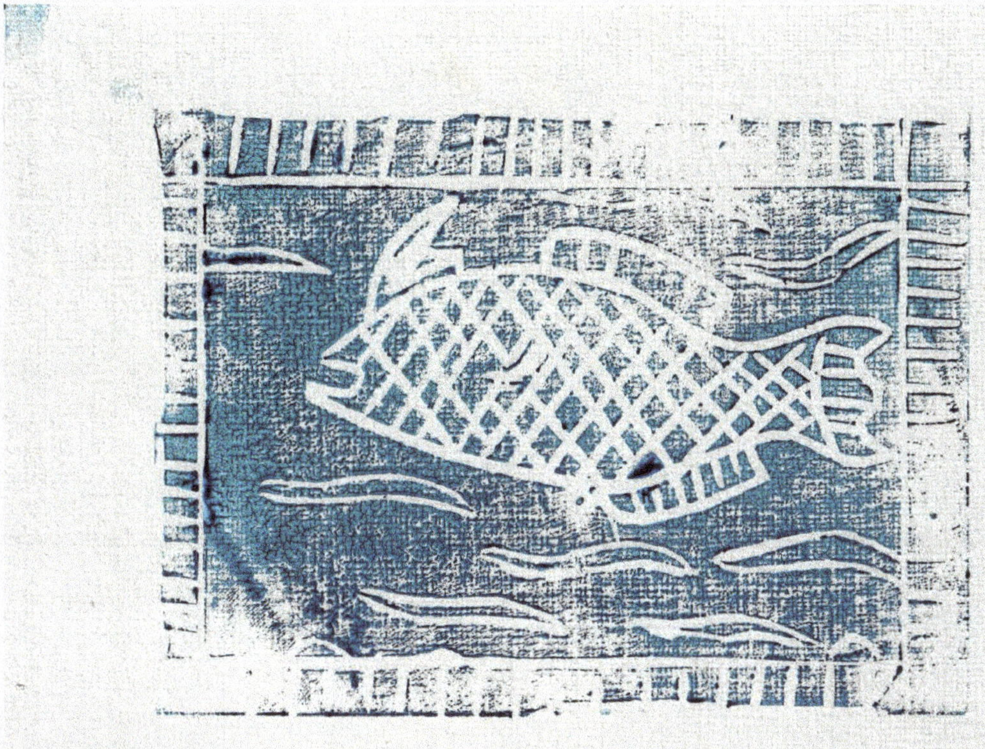

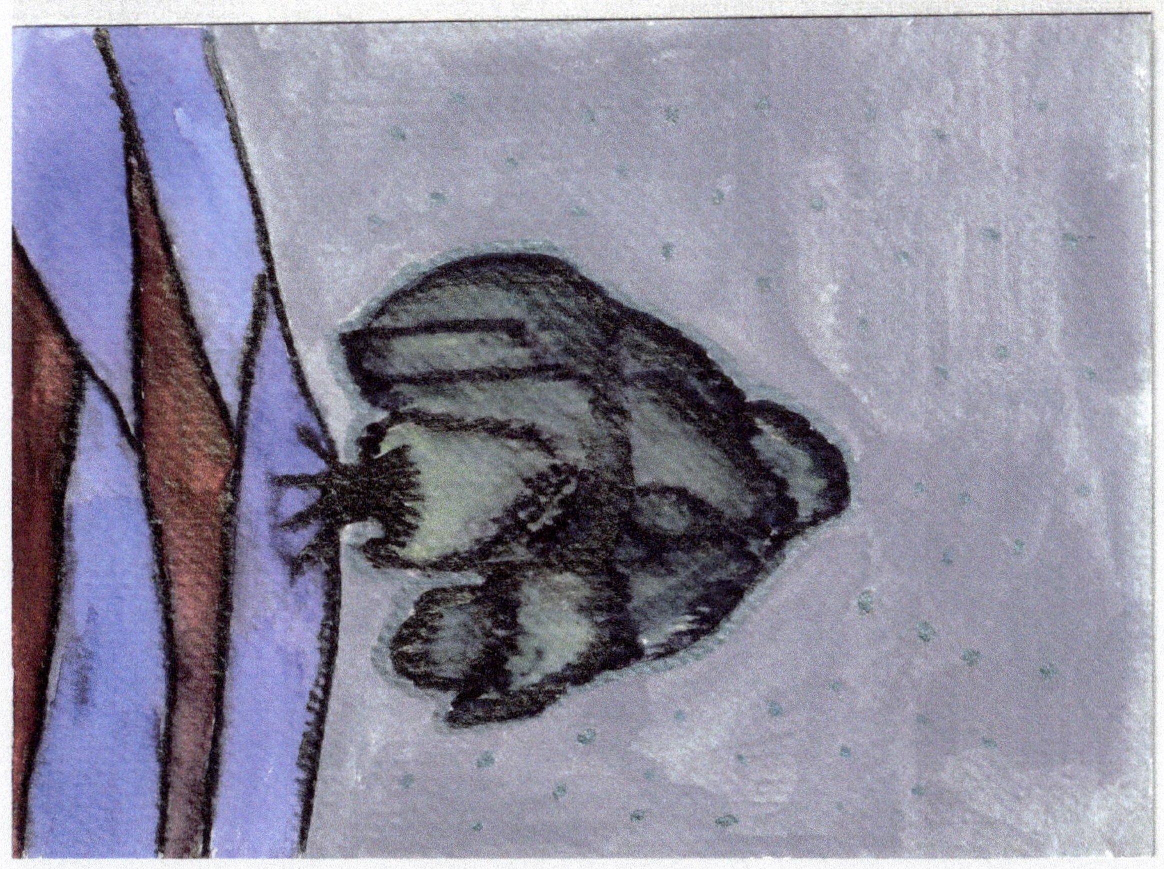

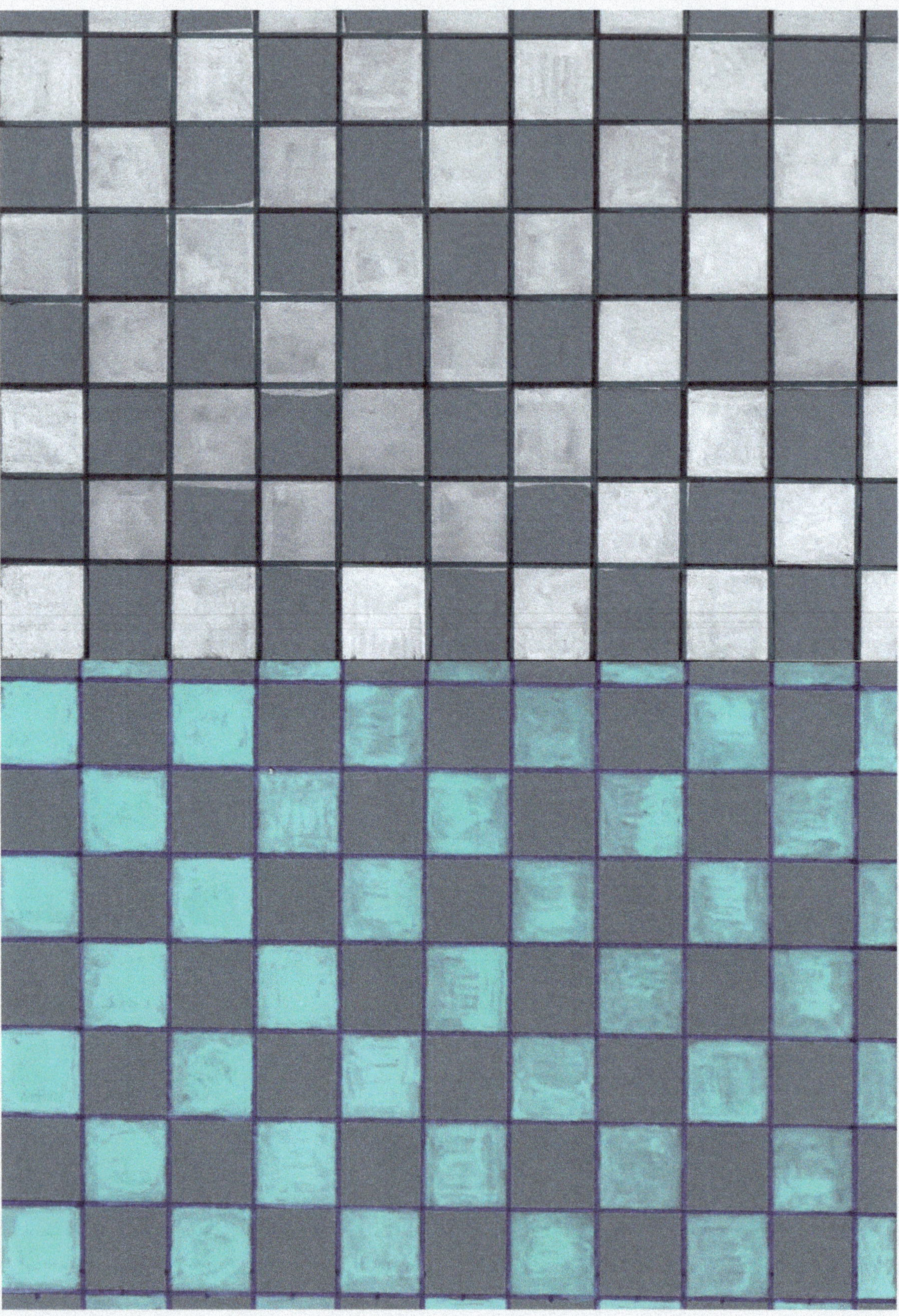

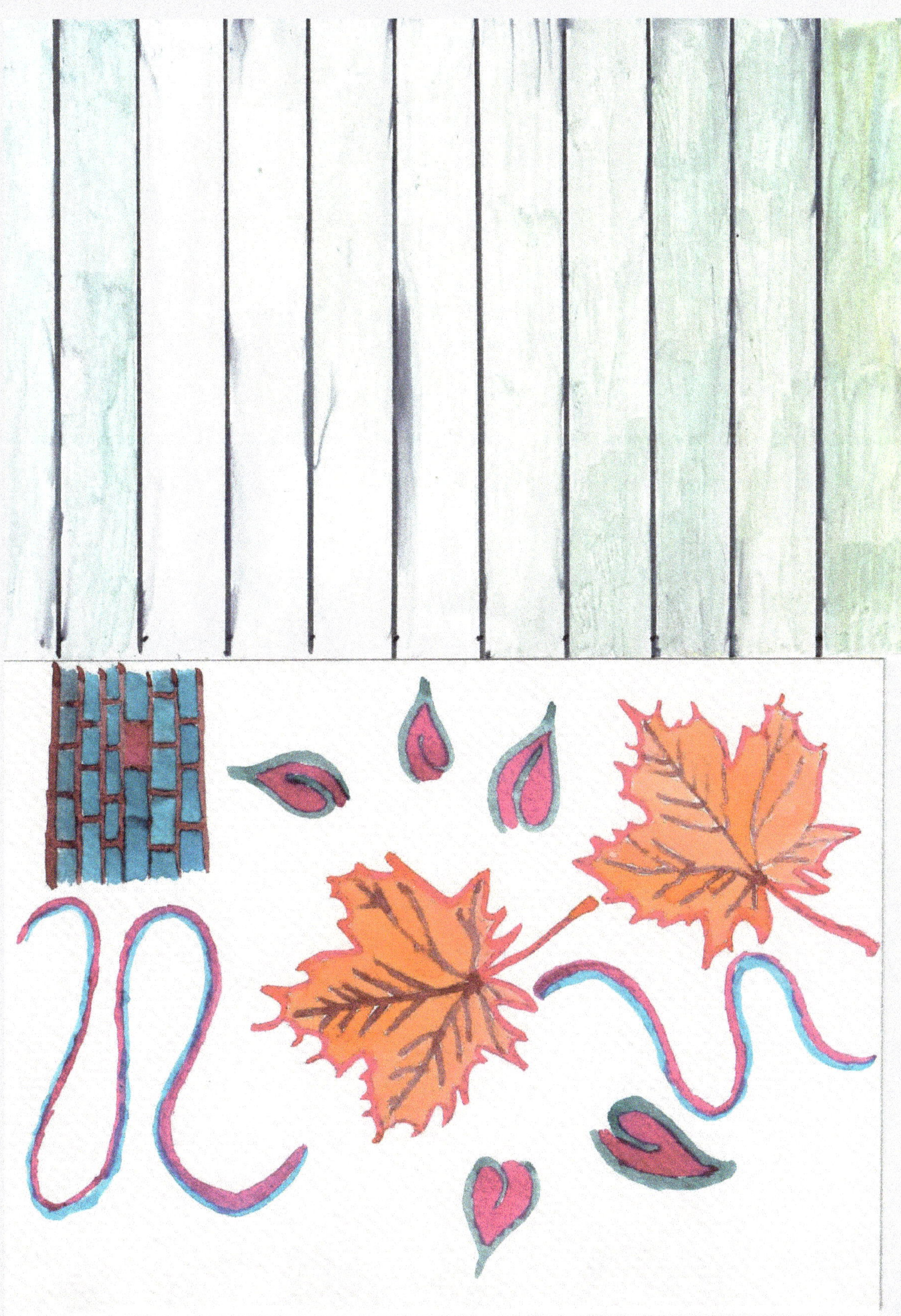

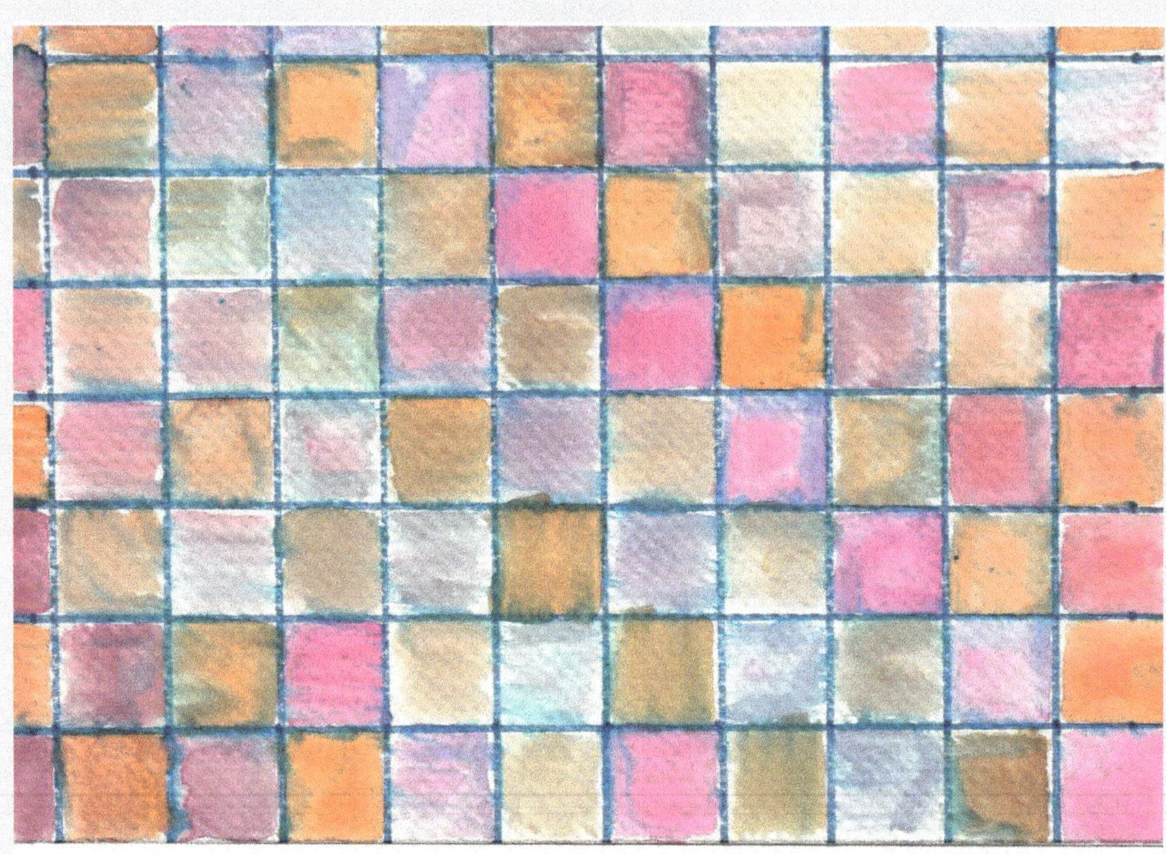

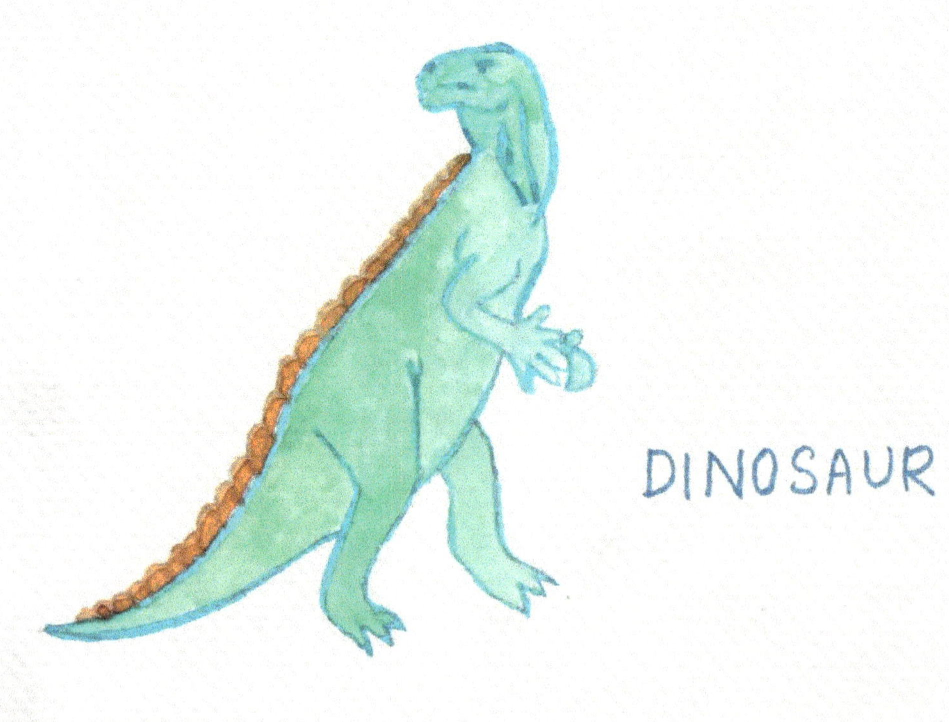
DINOSAUR

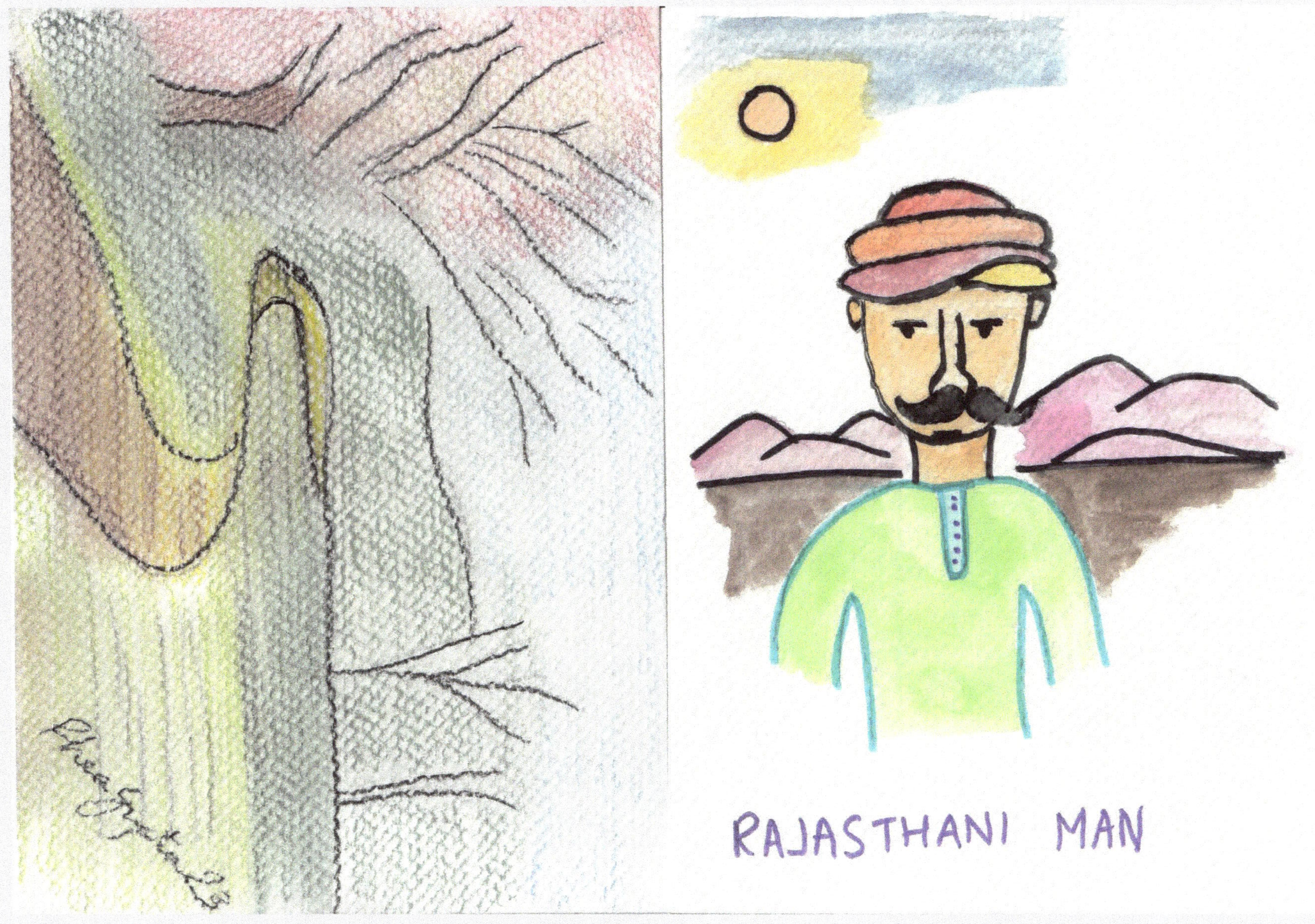
RAJASTHANI MAN

Thankyou